NoLex 12-12

PEACHTREE CITY
PLAN TO STAY™

Dante

Poet, Author, and Proud Florentine

Dante

Poet, Author, and Proud Florentine

John C. Davenport

CHELSEA HOUSE
PUBLISHERS
A Haights Cross Communications Company ®
Philadelphia

COVER: Dante and his poem, in front of the Duomo, in Florence, Italy.

CHELSEA HOUSE PUBLISHERS
VP, NEW PRODUCT DEVELOPMENT Sally Cheney
DIRECTOR OF PRODUCTION Kim Shinners
CREATIVE MANAGER Takeshi Takahashi
MANUFACTURING MANAGER Diann Grasse

Staff for Dante
EXECUTIVE EDITOR Lee Marcott
EDITORIAL ASSISTANT Carla Greenberg
PRODUCTION EDITOR Noelle Nardone
COVER AND INTERIOR DESIGNER Keith Trego
LAYOUT 21st Century Publishing and Communications, Inc.

A Haights Cross Communications ✦ Company ®

www.chelseahouse.com

First Printing

9 8 7 6 5 4 3 2 1

Library of Congress Cataloging-in-Publication Data

Davenport, John, 1960–
    Dante: poet, author, and proud Florentine/John Davenport.
      p. cm.–(Makers of the Middle Ages and Renaissance)
    Includes bibliographical references and index.
    ISBN 0-7910-8634-8 (hard cover)
    1. Dante Alighieri, 1265–1321. 2. Authors, Italian–To 1500–
Biography–Juvenile literature. I. Title. II. Series.
  PQ4335.D38 2005
  851'.1–dc22
                                          2005007492

CONTENTS

The Flames of Hell, the Promise of Paradise

As Dante Alighieri's pen came down and touched the paper, the ink began to flow. With each stroke, the black liquid spelled out another letter, another word. "I cannot well say," he had the narrator of his story remark, "whatever moment it was I began to blunder off the true path." [1] Dante paused there, for a second, to

1

think about all the mistakes he had made in his life. Over the years, he had experienced many ups and downs. So much had happened. Some of it had been good, but much of it had been bad. Now, as a middle-aged man, he recalled having seen his share of disappointment and heartbreak throughout his life. In fact, he could scarcely remember the last time he had felt any real joy. Perhaps he had experienced joy way back when he fell in love as a boy. Maybe the hours spent walking through his hometown had brought him joy. Those things, however, had happened a long time ago. They were ancient history, Dante thought to himself. There had been too many days filled with tragedy since then. Too many times, he had been betrayed and abandoned, allowing him to write with such skill and precise detail about hell.

Dante Alighieri knew pain, all too well. He had suffered through great trials that had tested his courage and fortitude. He tried to be a good, honest man through it all, but that was always hard for Dante, because he imagined the world was full of scheming, deceitful people. The book he was writing now, a work he entitled *The Inferno*, reflected his

DANTES DI ALEGIERIS FLORETINI

Dante Alighieri, born in 1265, loved his home city of Florence, Italy. That love turned to pain, however, when Dante was exiled from his beloved city by corrupt, greedy men.

vision of what life was really like. *The Inferno* was actually a metaphor. Hell was Dante's Italy; more specifically, it was his hometown of Florence, the source of many of his problems. Florence, Italy, was a beautiful, but corrupt city in the early 1300s. Dante Alighieri, nonetheless, had dedicated his life to his home city. He loved Florence and never hid his feelings. The city, however, eventually rejected this devoted son in favor of crude, greedy men. These men, so Dante felt, had no virtue, no loyalty, and no honor—only ambition. They did nothing to lift the city up. Their plots and maneuverings, Dante convinced himself, only dragged the city down. Now Dante took his revenge in the pages of his book. He depicted Florence as being evil. He placed his enemies in the tormenting flames of the afterlife.

On and on he wrote. Alone in a "great waste-land,"[2] Dante's main character met the famous Roman poet Virgil who promised to lead the traveler on a fearful journey. "I will be your guide," Virgil said, "to hear the cries of despair, and to behold ancient tormented spirits. . . ."[3] Ancient and tormented, that was exactly how Dante Alighieri felt. He could wipe the ink from his pen, but never the tears from his eyes. Florence, his lovely home city, had exiled him. City officials had accused him of a crime he did not commit, and had forced him to leave. He was told never to come back. Dante Alighieri was a man without a home. Regardless of what else was happening, Dante's mind always drifted back to his undeserved exile. He loved Florence, and always would. With equal passion, however, he hated the men who had lined up against him. The lies of fellow Florentines had driven him far from home. Dante found it impossible to forget, let alone forgive, their misdeeds.

Back at work, Dante picked up his pen and went to the inkwell once more. Each line seemed to come to his mind more quickly than the one before. He could barely keep up with his imagination, as he transformed his life into words. First the narrator, who was also his main character, would travel through hell. Here he would see all those wicked Italians get their just rewards. Those men had triumphed for a brief time, but they would suffer for eternity. Next he would begin the long, slow climb upward toward heaven. Purgatory would be his next stop. In this place, eager souls waited for

In Dante's vision of hell, those trapped there were forever joined, condemned to circle forever, like a flock of birds. Dante is shown here with the souls that have been transformed into birds.

their turn to enter heaven. After a pass through purgatory, the main character would end up in paradise. During this strange journey, Virgil, his Roman guide, would urge him on and give him the confidence to struggle upward. Virgil promises the man that if his "ascent continues," his next companion will be "one worthier than I." Only someone very special could be worthier than the great Virgil. "When I must leave you," Virgil explains, "you will be with her." [4]

Virgil was speaking about Dante's only true love—Beatrice. Years before Dante had settled down to write *The Inferno*, she had died, while still young and happy. Dante had known and loved her since childhood. He had followed her around Florence like a lost puppy. Every day, he traced her steps, hoping for a chance encounter. Young Dante, while growing up, prayed for just one sweet smile from Beatrice. She occupied his every thought. Then suddenly she was gone. Like the trust of his fellow Florentines, Beatrice was also torn away from Dante too soon. Her death left him alone and adrift. Without her to anchor his emotions, Dante felt lost.

Similar to his feelings about the Florence of his boyhood, Dante's memories of Beatrice endured. She would live on in Dante's mind, if nowhere else. He would always see her lovely face in his imagination. As much as Dante was hurt by the death of his first love, his memories of her allowed him to struggle on in life. Just as he waited for the day he could return to Florence, Dante also looked forward to the moment in time when he and Beatrice would come together in heaven. In the pages of *The Inferno,* Virgil said that such a time would come. The Roman poet guaranteed a joyous reunion. Beatrice would be Dante's guide to paradise, as the author escaped his own personal hell in late-medieval Italy.

Beatrice, Florence, the fires of eternal punishment, all of these images swirled around in Dante's head as he labored to make his pen speak for him. Dante wrote because he could never find the spoken words to express his inner feelings. Only with paper in front of him, did Dante have any hope of releasing some of the anger, sorrow, and frustration that boiled inside his heart. Life just never seemed to work out for him. Dante believed that everything always went wrong. His first love had died before he ever got the chance to tell her that he loved her. His native city had thrown him out. He had been forced to wander around Italy like some kind of beggar. Now he was writing a book that he was not even sure would be published. Trouble seemed to be his only companion.

Still Dante nurtured a tiny flame of hope deep in his heart, as he dipped the nib of his pen into the inkwell again. The pen moved with quick, bold strokes, tracing out more words and sentences. Dante's life would get better, just as it had for his main character in *The Inferno*. This man, if not Dante himself, knew that there would come a day when all his problems would melt away. God's "kingdom, His city, His seat of awe," Dante scribbled excitedly, awaited him in the next world. "Happy is the soul he chooses for that place."[5] There, in God's green garden, Dante's main character would find peace and everlasting love. He would discover a city that never betrayed anyone. Heaven did not exile just and virtuous men, as Florence seemed prone to do. Better yet, God's promise of a reunion with Beatrice meant an end to a lifetime of loneliness. The main character, and through him, Dante, would live in paradise with "her" for eternity.

Dante saw his life, as his pen floated across the paper in front of him. What began as trouble and turmoil in Italy would someday end in the joy of heaven. That was how Dante saw it; that was how he wrote. Plagued by constant difficulty, yet never losing hope, Dante became one of history's greatest writers. One of Dante's earliest admirers, Boccacio, called Dante a man "given to our age by the special grace of God."[6] Perhaps those words were true, but Dante himself never thought in those terms. He simply got along, as best as he could. He tried not to look too closely at the problems that constantly arose. Along the way, he produced one masterpiece after another. Dante, in the end, added to Western literature in so many ways. Among the most important of his contributions were the images of hell and heaven he created, especially hell. When most people today think of the punishment that awaits evildoers in the next life, they think of those unfortunate souls being in the place Dante described. Innumerable writers, throughout the centuries, have tried to imitate the great writer's style. They, however, were not Dante.

Dante Alighieri transformed his personal struggles into a grand story of humankind's salvation. He made the politics of a single Italian city-state, Florence, a lesson in how not to run an honest government, and how not to treat good and loyal citizens. He allowed his readers to connect their daily lives to the power of eternity, in a new and exciting way. Everything has consequences, Dante seemed to say, so be careful. More than anything else, however, Dante's message was one of perseverance and hope. Never stop climbing out of whatever hole you find yourself in. Keep climbing to the top.

The sheer simplicity and elegance of this advice still applies today. Whether in school, at work, or in one's community, Dante spoke to people about bringing an enduring optimism into the public and private aspects of life. This prescription, not to mention the sheer majesty of his words, made a legend out of a humble Florentine poet—the man we call Dante.

Test Your Knowledge

1 In writing *The Inferno*, Dante used hell as a metaphor for what?
   a. Roman politicians
   b. The Catholic Church
   c. The literature of the Renaissance
   d. Corruption in his home city of Florence

2 In *The Inferno*, who guides the narrator through hell?
   a. The devil
   b. Dante himself
   c. The Roman poet Virgil
   d. The Greek philosopher Plato

3 What role does Dante hope his beloved Beatrice will play in *The Inferno*?
   a. She will mourn those who die young.
   b. She will guide the narrator toward paradise.
   c. She will suffer eternal torment for betraying Dante.
   d. She will guide lost souls through purgatory.

4 How did Dante think *The Inferno* would be received?
   a. He knew it would be a huge success.
   b. He believed it would anger the Catholic Church.
   c. He was not sure it would ever be published.
   d. He never intended the work for publication.

5 What was the overall message of Dante's writing?

  a. All people will be judged in the afterlife.

  b. One should never stop trying to overcome adversity.

  c. People are basically evil.

  d. Damnation awaits all humankind.

ANSWERS: 1. d; 2. c; 3. b; 4. c; 5. b

Dante's Italy

In the late thirteenth century, Italy was just beginning to awaken from its medieval sleep. Since the fall of Rome in the fifth century, Italians had been confused. Their world had collapsed with the fall of Rome. Now they were struggling to put it all back together, and it would be a difficult job. Rome had given its empire shape and form. It had guided Europe, in particular Italy, for almost five centuries. Rome's absence left a big empty space in the middle of the Western world, and Italy was perhaps hardest hit. Nobody seemed able to fill the empty space once occupied by the grand Roman rulers. Power passed from one set of leaders to another. For the first few hundred years after Roman rule, Italy was controlled by a series of barbarian kings. Next local nobles and warlords took over. They should have ruled better than the foreigners, but they did not. Instead of taking care of the people, the nobles looked out only for themselves. They formed armed associations to protect their own interests. These groups constantly fought among themselves. According to one historian, by the late "twelfth century the [Italian] nobility was torn by homicidal rivalries."[7] In their spare time, the nobles bullied local people and made their lives more difficult. Everybody was fearful. Warlords and their friends were the only people to benefit.

In the end, none of these arrangements worked very well. Most common people were dissatisfied. They wanted a say in the workings of their government. In some places, people came together into communes. The communes were supposed to be run by the average citizens, and sometimes they were. Occasionally, however, wealthy men took charge. They acted like dictators and hurt the community as much as the violent nobles had. There had to be a better way, many thought. After a while, people started looking for government models that worked. By the year 1200, Italians began to experiment with new political systems.

While Italy's citizens tried out different political systems, Italy's city-states continued to grow in size and power, gradually becoming more important. In general, Italians looked more and more to city leaders for guidance. City-states, as a result, played a large role in the process of putting Italy back on track. Each of the city-states had it own special needs, of course. Each city-state wanted a system designed especially for its needs. In the end, many different types of governments emerged. Some governments were controlled by councils, some by one man, and others by the citizens themselves. Yet, no matter which system was in power, one thing became crystal clear. Cities became a bigger part of Italy's life and society.

AN URBAN ITALY

During the last decades of the 1200s, Italian city-states began to bustle with activity, as did the surrounding villages and towns. Italy was emerging from a long period of lethargy. As trade and manufacturing expanded, wealth began to grow. Urban craftsmen made beautiful and popular items that would be sold in faraway lands. City merchants ran thriving businesses. Urban bankers loaned money for shipping and the establishment of overseas colonies. Northern Italy was particularly busy with such activities. Cities such as Venice, Genoa, Milan, Pisa, and Dante's beloved Florence became wealthier with each passing year.

The Italian people could almost feel the positive energy in the air. Men and women felt proud of the accomplishments of their city-states. Average Italians, according to one writer, were "gaining a sense of power. The little people, as they were called—mechanics, tradesmen, and the like—were organizing themselves, and growing strong enough" to rule themselves.[8] Political systems arose to reflect this new strength. The Italian people, especially average workers referred to as the *popolino*, wanted more say in their own government. They added their calls for representation to those of the middle class. The *cives,* as the members of the middle class were known, clamored for a voice in city decisions. Over time, all of this clamoring paid off. Actual republics emerged and representatives of the people began to rule and pass laws.

As life began to improve, Italians became freer and better off. The cities became stronger, and no city-state, it was said, "made more rapid and steady progress than Florence."[9] Florence, with its broad avenues, ornate churches, and stunning *palazzos,* or palaces, stood out. The beauty of Florence's architecture set it apart. Many other Italian city-states tried to imitate the grandeur of Florence. In politics, too, Florence led the way. Perhaps nowhere else, did the citizens of a city-state have more power than in Florence.

Florence had genuine popular representation. Its people were active in their own government. Everybody was expected to take an active part in civic life. Citizens were expected to be more concerned about Florence than about their own needs. Civic virtue took hold, as honesty and public service were

The Palazzo della Signoria was the town hall of Florence in Dante's time. Its massive, stone military fortification projects the image of an urban fortress. The city and governmental identity are expressed through the tower of the palazzo.

taken for granted. The ideal city-state was one in which all of the inhabitants, wealthy or impoverished, acted on the principles of civic virtue. The people's representatives were expected to do the same. The government was charged with the responsibility of acting in the best interest of all citizens. The citizens, being equal members of the community, were expected to watch over the government and to serve the city. Florence, of course, was not a democracy as is understood today. Nonetheless popular government and an awareness of individual worth were beginning to shape its future.

Florence, in fact all of Dante's Italy, was certainly moving forward, but there was still a long way to go. People worked hard to make their dreams, including wealth and freedom, come true. No one, however, believed that success would come easily or quickly. In many places, Italy remained in the grip of violence and turmoil. Italians shared neither a common sense of direction nor a sense of self. Each city-state charted its own course and no two city-states were ever the same. Rivalries between ancient families and clans served only to highlight these differences. Violent confrontations between warring factions kept Italy fragmented, and made progress difficult. It was difficult to move forward when citizens were hurting and killing one another. Despite the fact that Italians desperately craved a better life, hatred and fighting prevented it from becoming a reality.

THE CURSE OF VIOLENCE

The Italian peninsula was torn by violence in the thirteenth century. Feuds raged between families seeking power. These fights often grew large enough to be considered civil wars. The most famous of these was a nearly 100-year war between the Guelphs and the Ghibellines. These two families battled for decades. The issues separating the two factions changed over time, but still they went on killing each other. Over time, the two sides even forgot what had started the war in the first place. Many city-states suffered through long periods of Guelph-Ghibelline combat, but Florence in particular, saw more than its share of the fighting. The war between these two groups raged there and eventually involved all of Florence. No one in the city could ignore the bloodshed. The conflict set "armed house against armed house, neighborhood against neighborhood." [10] The violence in Florence finally ended after a Guelph victory in 1266, the year after Dante Alighieri was born.

The latter years of the Middle Ages also saw personal violence like never before. "On a local level," one writer commented, "late-thirteenth-century northern Italy . . . was in constant turmoil." [11] Vendettas, private wars of revenge, caused blood to flow and made city streets unsafe. The proud Italian

Murder on a Bridge

Dante's Italy suffered through a great deal of violence. As far back as most people could remember, Italians had been settling disputes with clubs and knives. One incident in particular, which took place in 1216, was well known to Dante. Early in the morning, on a bridge in Florence, a young boy was attacked by a group of men. He was riding across the bridge when the attackers pulled him off his horse. They dragged the boy to the ground and viciously stabbed him to death. What had the boy done? The dead boy had made the mistake of insulting a powerful Florentine family. He had promised to marry one of the daughters in the family, but backed out at the last moment. He had families of the era were easily insulted. All too often, people settled disputes with knives and clubs. Murder led to murder. Friends and acquaintances were dragged into the fighting simply because they knew one of the warring families. Every city-state in Italy experienced such trouble. Parts of Florence in particular, began to resemble a battleground. Gangs terrorized people by launching "murderous attacks and counterattacks." [12] Fear made daily life difficult.

found a prettier girl from another family, so he was killed. It did not help that the two families involved were bitter political enemies. No one in Dante's Italy worked very hard at separating their public and private lives. A personal insult was avenged. It should have ended there, but it went on. The dispute between the families continued for years. Sometimes it moved into the political arena. At other times, it erupted into bloody street battles. These were just two of the many warring groups at the time. Florence, like the rest of Italy, was filled with violence. The murder at the bridge would not be the last. The social and political troubles that became a part of life in Dante's Italy had just begun.

Italy was rediscovering itself, but real rebirth would have to wait for peace.

Civil wars and feuds were only part of Italy's problems. Rising rates of poverty also led to unrest. Members of the wealthy Italian elite took whatever they wanted, without any concern for those below them. Huge villas rose up across the countryside. Tall mansions towered above many city neighborhoods. In cities such as Florence and Venice, wealthy men defended themselves with lies. They hid their real intentions, while claiming to have the interests of everybody at heart. These men created grand myths about themselves. They said that they were "unified, patriotic, and self-denying." [13] In truth, however, they simply wanted more wealth. Money was what they craved, and they used their power to get as much of it as they could.

The Italian elite grew wealthier with successes in trade and business. Wealthy men got even wealthier by acting as landlords. Many bought and rented out land. Tenant farmers, who usually lived in poverty and always feared eviction, worked farms controlled by the elite. The urban poor suffered as well. Their houses were small and cramped. Their streets were

In the mid-1200s, Florence was a city divided. While rising rates of poverty led to unrest, the wealthy simply acquired more riches. This gold coin, known as a Florent, bears the coat of arms of Florence.

narrow and dirty. Few people had enough food or clean water. Sickness and hunger tore apart many families. Many times, even fairly successful trades-men, artisans, and shopkeepers barely got by. Misery

lingered at the fringes of society, ready to strike anyone at anytime.

In the end, for all its loveliness and promise,
Dante's Italy was a hard, cold, complex, and sometimes bloody place to live. Italy, especially Florence,
was a busy society caught in a wave of often unset-
tling change. It was a place of genuine contrasts.
Italians could be creative and destructive at once.
They could be wonderful and horrible. Here in the
middle of all this confusion, a man named Alighiero
Alighieri and his wife, Bella, raised a son named
Dante. Dante Alighieri was a cute little baby who
would be a famous poet one day. Along the way,
however, he would also experience great sadness
and disappointment.

Test Your Knowledge

1 After the fall of Rome, what were conditions like in Italy?
   a. Barbarian kings took control.
   b. Local nobles and warlords vied for power.
   c. Communes arose, but were frequently controlled by wealthy men.
   d. All of the above.

2 Which of the following is true of the Italian city-states in Dante's time?
   a. They encouraged tradesmen and merchants.
   b. They forbade banking within their boundaries.
   c. They suppressed global exploration.
   d. They isolated themselves from the rest of Europe.

3 Florence was renowned among other Italian city-states
   a. for its economic development.
   b. for its beautiful and elaborate architecture.
   c. for its corruption.
   d. for its rivers.

4 In the years just before Dante's birth, violent family rivalries and civil wars tore through Italy. The most famous of these was
   a. the War of the Roses.
   b. the Napoleonic Wars.
   c. the Hundred Years' War.
   d. none of the above.

5   What effect did Italy's civil wars and feuds have on
    city-states like Florence?
    a. The conflicts sped economic development and
       invention.
    b. Other countries took the opportunity of unrest
       to invade Italy.
    c. A socialist movement swept the country.
    d. A wealthy elite gained power at the expense of
       the general population.

ANSWERS: 1. d; 2. a; 3. b; 4. c; 5. d

A Birth in Florence

Dante Alighieri, referred to by one writer as "this special glory of Italy," was born in the late spring of 1265.[14] He was born into a good family, known for its honor and honesty. People respected the Alighieris. Dante's family could even be called distinguished, in a way. His father, Alighiero Alighieri, came from a long line of proud warriors. There were, indeed, some strong men in Dante's family. All of Dante's ancestors, in fact, were renowned for their courage and determination. They had a reputation for standing up for what they believed in. Dante's ancestors held strong opinions, no matter how much trouble those opinions caused them. Dante followed in their footsteps.

Dante's family history was full of men and women who were willing to fight for their values. They gave themselves over to lives of public service. Dante's great-grandfather, for example, was an imperial knight. In his shining armor, he fought bravely for the Holy Roman Empire. He served his country and his church at the expense of his own life. Dante took pride in the fact that his great-grandfather had made the ultimate sacrifice for his homeland. He had died in battle during the Second Crusade.

Dante's father, Alighiero Alighieri, was just as tough as his ancestors, but he lived a quiet life. He could have bragged and boasted, and used his family name to gain favor, yet he chose a more humble existence. Alighiero Alighieri was not weaker than those who came before him. He simply applied his energy in other ways. While not a warrior, Alighiero Alighieri was single-minded in his devotion to his work and his family. He worked hard, and provided for his wife and children, as a banker and a landlord. A family man, Alighiero Alighieri kept to himself and never called attention to his deeds. In fact, he tried to be just a regular Florentine. In the end, however, according to one writer, he was "destined, more through his son than himself, to become famous." [15]

Alighiero Alighieri thought things through carefully, and rarely made bad choices. One of his worst decisions, though, was choosing to side with the Guelphs in the 1250s. When the Ghibellines defeated the Guelphs and took power in Florence in 1260, Alighiero Alighieri had to watch his step. It would have been very easy for the new leadership to brand him an enemy of the city. For the next six years, Dante's father did everything possible to stay out of trouble. His years of self-imposed inactivity ended in 1266, however, when the Guelphs over-whelmed the Ghibellines during the Battle of Benevento. The new Guelph government looked

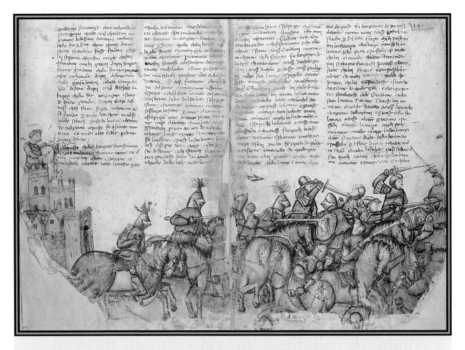

The battle between the Ghibellines of Siena and the Guelphs of Florence is depicted here. One of Alighiero Alighieri's worst decisions was choosing to side with the Guelphs in the 1250s.

much more favorably upon Alighiero Alighieri and his family.

Perhaps Alighiero Alighieri was allowed to remain in Florence during the Ghibelline years because he was married to the daughter of a former Ghibelline leader. His wife, Bella degli Albati, came from an established and respected family. She was wealthy, well educated, and had solid political connections. She was a good match for Alighiero Alighieri. She loved him, and always remained loyal, no matter what happened. She was the type of woman Alighiero Alighieri needed. She was also a wonderful mother to baby Dante. From his birth in 1265 until the day she died, Dante's mother tried to shield the little boy from every misfortune. She tried to make sure that nothing disturbing, such as turbulent Florentine politics, ever touched his life. Dante's mother wanted him to grow up happy, in a positive environment.

Given all of the turmoil in Florence at the time, growing up in a peaceful, positive environment could prove difficult. When fighting had broken out early in 1266, no one was sure who would end up governing the city. When the Guelph victory at Benevento settled the matter once and for all, roles were reversed in the Alighieri household. Bella's marriage to Alighiero protected her from Guelph revenge. No one could touch her, or Dante. Alighiero Alighieri made sure of it.

The Alighieri family became part of the new, accepted group in Florence. Free from Ghibelline suspicion and again on the winning side, Alighiero

Alighieri prospered. His family thrived, and grew larger, with the addition of more children. Dante's father moved the growing family into a bigger house

A Boy Named Durante

The baby boy born to Alighiero and Bella Alighieri already had a last name. It would be Alighieri, of course. The real issue was choosing the first name. Alighiero Alighieri told his wife to name her little boy whatever she wanted. Thinking hard, she finally came up with a name she really liked. She decided to name her son Durante. That had been her grandfather's name. Her boy would grow up with a strong sense of family history. His first and last names would remind him of his mother and father every day of his life. Someday the tiny baby would be proud to say, "I am Durante Alighieri." Over the course of the following year, however, a slight change was made. The little Alighieri boy's name was shortened. His name was called by his parents so often, that a few letters got dropped. By the time he was baptized, everyone was calling Durante by a new name. It stuck, and he was baptized with it. Alighiero and Bella Alighieri's son's name was recorded as Dante Alighieri.

in Florence's best neighborhood. In fact, Dante's childhood home was located in Florence's fanciest *sestiere*, or sixth of the city.

As his businesses grew, Alighiero Alighieri invested in land. Like other men of that time with a little money, he purchased some tracts of land outside of Florence's city walls, and rented them to small farmers. Alighiero Alighieri, however, was more honest and fair than the average landlord. His land was located in a very lovely countryside. Rolling hills and green fields gave the land a peaceful, dreamlike quality. Alighiero Alighieri and his family cherished their rural property. Little Dante, in particular, loved to explore the family land. He would walk or sometimes sit for hours, taking in the picturesque vistas. The land, for him, came to symbolize the quiet beauty of a well-lived life.

DISRUPTIONS, BAD AND GOOD

Everything seemed perfect to young Dante. The serenity of those early years, however, ended abruptly in 1272, when his mother died unexpectedly. Dante had been unusually close to his mother. Her death caused him great pain. Dante missed her very much, but Alighiero Alighieri's grief was even deeper. He had cherished his wife. She had given his life direction and purpose. He was lost without her. Yet he knew he had to go on. Lesser men might have let their heartbreak overwhelm them, but not Alighiero Alighieri. He came from strong stock, and he knew that now was not the time for self-pity. He had a family to think of and, he felt, a family must have a mother. In this, Alighiero Alighieri's attitude was typical for his day and age. He simply assumed that a man and his children required the guidance and support of a woman. So, not too long after his wife's death, he remarried. With his new wife, Alighiero Alighieri patched together his broken life and home. Love blossomed and the couple had children of their own, one boy and two girls. Dante quickly formed strong bonds with his half brother and half sisters. Dante, it seemed, was every bit as tough as his father.

Yet, just as the family was settling into a routine, Dante's life was changing again, this time with the excitement of love. Each year in May, Florence held its annual spring festival. All the young boys and girls of the city attended. The festival was, in fact, a celebration of youth and new beginnings. Spring was thought of as a time for fresh starts and restored hope. Young people took center stage, and their families, not surprisingly, sensed a golden opportunity. With all the boys and girls in one place, parents seized the opportunity to shop around for suitable marriage partners for their children. There was no better time than the spring celebration to see just who might be available to marry in a few years. Among other things, the annual spring festival brought young people and adults together in an atmosphere of love and hope.

Social calls were common during the festival. Florentines enjoyed getting together and talking, and the festival provided the perfect opportunity to visit with neighbors, invite them over for dinner, and discuss how they could help each other. For Dante and his father, this tradition meant an invitation to the home of Falco Portinari. Portinari was a rich and powerful man who held a great deal of influence in Florentine politics. Although many men in his position were corrupt, Portinari was an honest man. He was also famous for his kindness and generosity. Falco Portinari never missed an opportunity to help those in need. He built hospitals for the sick and gave money to the poor.

Dante respected Falco Portinari and tried to concentrate on paying him full attention during the visit. Concentration proved impossible, however. Dante simply could not focus on what his host was saying. He was not rude, just distracted. Dante was busy staring at Portinari's daughter. She was incredible. Dante's heart pounded and his head was in a swirl when he saw Beatrice Portinari for the first time. She was so lovely and charming that Dante immediately became convinced she was "no child of mortal man but of God." [16] Another biographer described Beatrice Portinari as "very graceful for her age . . . full of such pure loveliness that many thought her almost a little angel." [17] Dante himself recalled how she "appeared humbly and properly dressed" for her age, but stunning nonetheless. [18] There was no doubt about it, Dante was in love.

IN THE NAME OF LOVE

Over the next four years, Dante never missed an opportunity to be near Beatrice Portinari. He even followed her to church, where he would sit, silently, in a nearby pew to watch her. His greatest joy came in simply being near her, but life went on, and Dante's head needed as much exercise as his heart. Whatever time was not spent chasing after Beatrice, Dante devoted to his studies. He loved to learn and he worked hard at school. Another of his biographers wrote that Dante "devoted himself not only to literature but to other liberal studies," as befitted "an excellent man." [19] He was known around his neighborhood for reading everything he could get his hands on. Dante's friends noticed that, despite many distractions, "none saw Dante move from his position, or once lift his eyes from his book." [20] Dante was so driven that he chose to study classic literature with one of the most famous writers of the day, Brunetto Latini.

Beatrice Portinari and the study of classical literature—Dante had all he needed. His life was comfortable. His mind was challenged and his heart was in love. Everything seemed perfect when, in 1277, Dante's father stunned the lovesick boy by announcing that a marriage had been planned for him. Alighiero Alighieri and the Donati family, wealthy neighbors, had agreed that Dante, when he was old enough, would marry a Donati daughter named Gemma. She was the same age as Dante and the marriage would help his father to form an important political connection. As was common at that time, Alighiero Alighieri had business and politics in mind, not affection. Dante, of course, thought otherwise. He had hoped to wed Beatrice Portinari someday. She was the girl he loved. She should be his bride. That dream became impossible now, however, and there was nothing Dante could do about it.

Fathers ruled Italian families in the thirteenth century much like kings ruled their kingdoms. They made all of the decisions about family business, and good connections took priority over trivial things, like love. An Alighieri-Donati union would help both families. Each would gain money, land, and influence. Equally important was the fact that a refusal to marry Gemma Donati would likely lead to bloodshed. Important men in Italian city-states were careful not to insult other important people. Men guarded their reputation and their honor dearly. A refusal of Germma Donati's hand would be a huge insult to the Donati family. It would send

This map of Florence shows Dante Alighieri's home next door to the home of the Donati family. Despite Dante's undying love for Beatrice Portinari, Gemma Donati would become Dante's wife.

the message that a Donati daughter was not fit to marry an Alighieri son. Such a message would not be tolerated. Vicious and long-lasting feuds over these kinds of slights were all too common in Dante's time.

Dante's father understood the importance of this union, as did young Dante. Dante also knew that his feelings were of no consequence. Love lost out to more practical, and public, considerations. For the good of his family, Dante Alighieri would marry Gemma Donati, whether he liked it or not. That, of course, meant that Dante could forget about ever being with Beatrice Portinari. He would never have his only true love. Dante's life seemed over before it had really started.

Test Your Knowledge

1 Dante's father was employed as
   a. an imperial knight.
   b. a banker and landlord.
   c. a poet and playwright.
   d. a sculptor and stonemason.

2 In 1272, Dante's childhood was disrupted by what event?
   a. The death of his mother
   b. War between the Ghibellines and the Guelphs
   c. A fire that destroyed the family's home
   d. None of the above

3 The young Dante met his beloved, Beatrice Portinari, during what event?
   a. A birthday party
   b. A church service
   c. The wedding of a friend
   d. The annual spring festival

4 During his youth, Dante acquired a reputation as
   a. a daydreamer.
   b. a lazy boy.
   c. a devoted student.
   d. none of the above.

5 In thirteenth-century Italy, arranged marriages
were seen as

a. an accepted social convention.

b. a way to build economic and social alliances.

c. a matter of family reputation and honor.

d. all of the above.

ANSWERS: 1. b; 2. a; 3. d; 4. c; 5. d

From Boyhood to Manhood

The late 1270s and early 1280s were busy and eventful years for Dante Alighieri. During this time, he was thrust into manhood. The most important time, however, was the year 1283. Dante Alighieri had experienced many ups and downs in his life, and each

45

time he had calmly accepted his fate, good or bad, and had gone on with his life. In 1283, however, Dante experienced perhaps the worst and best days of his life. Each event changed him forever. First his father died suddenly, of unknown causes, leaving Dante with no one to help him grow up. Next Beatrice Portinari finally acknowledged his presence. She actually spoke to him.

Dante's relationship with his father had been respectful and serious. As was common during the late Middle Ages, Dante's father was not his friend. He was more important than that. Alighiero Alighieri guided his son, taught him, and acted as the boy's model for manhood. Alighiero Alighieri's dignified manner was something Dante emulated. The boy patterned himself after a father he looked to for support and advice. The older man was his mentor. Now Dante had no one to turn to when he needed direction. He was on his own. At the age of 18, Dante became the head of his household. He took over his father's properties and assumed the burden of caring for his brothers and sisters. Dante became a man before he really knew how to be one.

FINDING A FATHER

Dante needed some help. He desperately needed someone to lay out a path for him to follow. Just such a figure appeared in the form of Dante's tutor, Brunetto Latini. Latini provided a strong male presence, and taught the boy how to develop and sharpen his writing. Dante already showed an interest in writing. Latini simply encouraged it to grow. Latini also helped Dante understand his role in society. He showed Dante how to act like a man, in private and in public. Latini taught Dante about civic duty and political responsibility. He offered his student a model of mature devotion to Florence. Dante learned every lesson and applied them all to his life. In short, under Latini's guidance, Dante grew up. He began his evolution into the man he would become— a great writer and a patriotic citizen of Florence.

Physically, the maturing Dante was nothing much to look at. Boccaccio remembered him as being "of moderate height [and] accustomed to walking some-what bowed. His face was long . . . and his eyes rather large than small." His mind, however, was already sharp. "None was more vigilant than he in study," Boccaccio wrote. Growing up, Dante also perfected his voice until "he was eloquent and fluent in speech."[21] Latini was responsible for much of this. He helped Dante channel and hone his talents. Nobody was better suited for the job than Latini.

Latini, an accomplished author, wrote books on many subjects. There seemed to be no end to what Latini was able to do. He put his pen and his mind to work on almost everything. Although he was capable of writing in both French and Italian, Latini's most famous works were in Italian. The best known of these books was his Italian translation of the ancient Greek philosopher Aristotle's book on ethics. Latini, a dedicated Guelph, loved Florence. Beginning in 1266, Latini became very active politically, but writing remained his passion. Latini's impact on Dante was so deep that the young man later said of his friend and teacher, he "taught me how man makes himself eternal." For giving him this gift, Dante felt that "while I live . . . [I] should show what gratitude I have for it."[22]

BEATRICE PORTINARI

Learning and writing did not stop Dante from pursuing more down-to-earth matters. Dante's

An Early Exile

Brunetto Latini got into trouble long before he became Dante's teacher and substitute father. Latini had always been active in politics. He enjoyed arguing about current events, and he was well informed, too. He knew a great deal about the ongoing dispute between the Guelphs and the Ghibellines. Latini made it clear to everyone that he supported the Guelphs. They would provide the best government for Florence, Latini argued. Public declarations of this sort were dangerous in late-medieval Italy, however. Power changed hands often. One day, people could be on the winning side. The next day, they could be among the losers. After the Battle of Monteperti, in 1260, Latini became one of the losers. The Ghibellines defeated the Guelphs at Monteperti, and began driving Guelph sympathizers from Florence. Latini would soon be a target, so he left Florence before the Ghibellines could get to him. He went to France, where he lived for the next six years, until the Guelphs regained power. Latini was in exile, but he used his time well. He published four books and a series of other pieces. Latini made exile a productive part of his life. He had a knack for making the best of things. It was a skill he would pass on to Dante.

attraction to Beatrice Portinari changed and matured. Despite being promised to Gemma Donati, Dante continued to have strong feelings for Beatrice. In fact, he never stopped thinking about her. His affection grew stronger after that wonderful day in May 1283, when Beatrice finally noticed him. As they passed one another on the street, Beatrice looked at Dante and said, "hello." It was not much, but it was more than enough for Dante. He later remarked that, at that very moment, he saw in Beatrice's "ineffable courtesy . . . all the terms of beatitude."[23] Simply stated, she made him feel like he was in heaven.

Dante could barely contain himself. A few words from Beatrice Portinari made his heart soar. Overjoyed, he immediately sat down and scribbled out a love poem. He soon had it published. Worshipping Beatrice Portinari from afar became Dante Alighieri's primary occupation. He worked hard and finished his studies under Latini, but his mind and heart were fixed on Beatrice. Still he could not forget that his marriage to Gemma Donati was fast approaching. When the day finally arrived in 1286, the marriage contract came due, and the young couple was wed in a small local church. Beatrice

Portinari remained Dante's first love, but now he had a wife. The very next year, Dante and Gemma had a baby, a boy they named Giovanni.

Dante could now claim full manhood. He was the head of his father's household; he had completed his education; and he was in love (even if the object of his affection was not his legal wife), and newly married. He also possessed a typically Florentine "love for honour and fame," and a deep devotion to his city.[24] In every way, Dante Alighieri was a real man in the eyes of his community. Perhaps most important, Dante had fulfilled all of the requirements for full citizenship, except one. Every male citizen was expected to serve in his city's army. Florentine men were required to prove the depth of their patriotism in battle. War was viewed as the true measure of civic virtue and public sacrifice. A good citizen, it was believed, cared more for his city than his own life. Serving in the military was the one duty Dante had not fulfilled. He moved quickly to change this.

SERVING FLORENCE IN WAR AND PEACE

Like many boys in Florence of his social class, Dante had received some military training. He had learned

Dante Alighieri's military training included learning
how to ride a horse and how to wear armor. This
bronze sculpture of a horseman is from the Museo
Nazionale del Bargello in Florence.

how to ride a horse, and how to maneuver it, as if in battle. He was also taught how to wear armor. Dante drilled with other youths and trained physically. Above all, he learned how to use a sword.

The time to test these skills came in 1289. At a place called Campaldino, Ghibelline forces from the city of Alezzo met to challenge the Florentine Guelphs. Dante joined the Guelph troops who rode out to confront the Ghibellines. He was ready for his first battle, and it could not have been more frightening. The Battle of Campaldino turned out to be a bloody confrontation. Dante, serving in the cavalry, was in the thick of the battle from the start. Both sides, Guelph and Ghibelline, fought hard. When the battle was over, in a stunning victory, the Florentine soldiers had killed some 1,700 enemy troops and captured some 3,000 men. Dante noted the ferocious fighting and claimed that, no matter how scary it was, the battle had confirmed his manliness. He wrote long after the battle that "I showed myself no child in armed warfare." He admitted that he "felt much fear [but] at the end great happiness at the outcome of the battle."[25] Biographer Lionardo Bruni Aretino summed up the

The courtyard of the Museo Nazionale del Bargello is shown here. The most famous stone palace of the city was built on commission in 1255, as a fortress and arsenal, to resist the nobles of the city.

episode by concluding simply that Dante "fought valiantly for his country on this occasion."[26]

The peace that followed the Battle of Campaldino was short-lived. Only weeks after the Florentine victory, rebels from the city of Pisa took control of an important castle. Dante, at the urging of a friend, joined the force sent by Florence to assist in retaking the fortress. He arrived with the rest of the army, and a siege began. The fighting lasted a mere ten days, but Dante had another battle to his credit.

Dante returned to Florence as a victorious warrior, but his military career had always been a temporary job, a way to prove his rightful claim to citizenship. He now had a worthy military record and a secure place in Florentine society. The next step in his journey would be to put down the warrior's weapons and serve Florence politically. A government office would soon be his. In this way, he could prove the depth and quality of his civic virtue. Everything should have been fine, but sorrow and grief soon darkened Dante's life.

Test Your Knowledge

1 Dante's tutor, Brunetto Latini, taught the young
   man
   a. how to develop and sharpen his writing.
   b. how to refine his singing voice.
   c. how to be mayor of Florence.
   d. how to be a wealthy businessman.

2 When did Dante's arranged marriage to Gemma
   Donati occur?
   a. 1291
   b. 1286
   c. 1289
   d. After he had finished writing *The Inferno*

3 Dante's brief period of military service was
   characterized by
   a. bravery in combat.
   b. his refusal to serve in combat.
   c. his promise to leave Florence.
   d. the end of the Hundred Years' War.

4 When the young Dante was not studying, what
   consumed his free time?
   a. His early plans to write *The Inferno*
   b. His adoration for Beatrice Portinari
   c. His desire to prove himself as a soldier
   d. His desire to have a family

5 In which battle did Dante fight?

a. The Battle of Pisa

b. The Roman-Florentine War

c. The Battle of Campaldino

d. None of the above

ANSWERS: 1. a; 2. b; 3. a; 4. b; 5. c

A Civic Life

Dante's first great disappointment in life came in 1287, when he received the news that his beloved Beatrice Portinari had married another man. His heart ached. The marriage forced Dante to admit to himself that he had "been hers ever since childhood."[27] Much worse news was yet to come. Beatrice Portinari's wedding had been a blow, but her sudden death in 1290 shook Dante to the core. She had been a part of his life for years. He simply took her presence for granted. In his mind, Beatrice Portinari would always be there to brighten his days. Now she was dead. Without warning, Dante's "most beautiful Beatrice . . . left the sufferings of this world."[28] Dante felt very alone.

Of course, Dante had his wife and his children, but Beatrice Portinari had been special. She had stood above everyone else in Dante's life. He might have known something terrible was about to happen. He had been having nightmares about Beatrice's death for a while, but he had forced himself not to pay attention to them. He was shattered when they actually came true. His existence seemed pointless. Life did not seem to have much meaning. He was thrown, as a later biographer wrote, "into such sorrow, and such grief and tears, that many of those nearest him . . . believed that death alone would end them."[29] Dante realized that his world, as he had known it, was finished. Beatrice Portinari's death pulled something from his heart that would never be replaced.

After grieving, Dante turned from his emotions, and relieved his pain in the only way he knew—he wrote. Working madly, Dante produced a book entitled *La Vita Nuova di Dante Alighieri* (*The New Life of Dante Alighieri*). The work was essentially a detailed account of his love for, and life around, Beatrice Portinari. He certainly did not say that outright. In Dante's time, writers expressed their personal feelings indirectly. They wrote in metaphor, or in little stories called allegories. That is what Dante did in *La Vita Nuova.* In its pages, Dante chronicled how he felt and what he experienced. His private thoughts and dreams, in other words, were put on public display in *La Vita Nuova.* The book's conclusion sent its readers a clear message. Dante ended by promising his audience that he would "write no more of this blessed one." If he lived long enough, however, someday he might "say of her what was never said of any woman."[30] Perhaps, Dante hinted, he might tell everyone what it was like to love an angel. Only with Beatrice Portinari safe in his memory, could the great poet move on into a new life, and in politics.

FROM LOVE TO POLITICS

Dante entered into civic life at the age of 30. He had never seriously thought of public life as being right for him, but a series of conversations with a friend convinced him otherwise. The friend urged Dante to go into politics, telling him how much he could do for Florence. Dante already believed that the future of his city depended upon honest men taking government positions. Florence needed true patriots, and Dante was convinced he was just the man for the job.

Dante was obviously a good man, but he still had to work his way up in politics, like everyone else. Anybody who wanted to serve his city had to begin at the lowest level of political activity, in a local guild. Dante knew the process, so he started his new career by joining a guild. Late-medieval guilds were formed by groups of likeminded men who did the same work. They were bound together by mutual respect and support. Guilds were also political clubs. Their members shared similar political beliefs and goals. Guilds were often very powerful, and had the ability to change public policy. They were the perfect place to learn the skills needed for government office.

Dante was aware of the power of the guilds when he joined his first one in 1295. It was not a particularly prominent guild, but that was not important. Dante's ego was far from inflated. In fact, when asked, he reported his profession simply as

Civitas

Civitas was the idea that a man owed his loyalty and service to his city. No matter where a citizen lived, civitas held; he owed that place his love and respect. If a citizen loved his city, he would put its interests before his own. Giving everything possible to the community, it was believed, made everybody's life better. This was a common assumption in Dante's Italy, part of a larger philosophy known as civic humanism. Civic humanists believed that, if a person devoted himself to his public service, he would help his city and earn the honor and appreciation of those around him. As one scholar wrote, selfless public service made for a good city, and "the good city was the only place for a man to live."* Dante very much thought this way. He prized Florence, above all else. Unfortunately, his love was not returned. Perhaps Dante should have learned a lesson from the example of Giano della Bella. He was a Florentine politician who

"Florentine poet." [31] For the next five years, Dante learned how to be a government leader. He learned all he could about running a city. He also honed his speaking and debating skills. Only after thorough preparation, did Dante finally decide "to pursue that

wanted to rid his city of people who took advantage of the city. He felt that if a citizen put his own needs before those of Florence, he should have no role in running the city. In 1293, Giano della Bella wrote a series of laws designed to exclude selfish nobles from the city government. The laws said that no noble or wealthy man could hold public office. Better yet for average Florentines, nobles were forced to respect common citizens. If a rich man bothered, for instance, a middle-class man, the penalty was severe: the rich man would have one hand chopped off. Giano della Bella wanted to clean out all the greedy, selfish Florentines. In the end, though, they got rid of him. His laws were repealed in 1295 and he was sent into exile.

* Alessandro Passerin d'Entrèves, "Civitas," in *Dante: A Collection of Critical Essays*, John Freccero, ed. Englewood Cliffs, NJ: Prentice-Hall, 1965, p. 143.

fleeting honor and false glory of public office."[32] He offered himself to Florence, and the city elected him prior in June 1300.

PUBLIC OFFICE

A prior acted as one of Florence's mayors, at the time. A man only held the post for two months, but it was a very prestigious job. Priors were viewed as representatives of the people. They safeguarded everyone, not just the elite. Dante felt real satisfaction in his election. He was proud of having been selected. Yet entering the public limelight opened Dante up to criticism from his political enemies. Many Florentines remembered his mother's Ghibelline connections. Some people looked at his personal history and questioned Dante's loyalty to the Guelph government. Others began plotting his downfall. Dante later claimed that all of his "troubles and hardships had their cause rise" in his election to city office.[33] It would seem he was right.

Dante worked hard to balance his public life and his personal life. He even moved his family next door to his office, in order to be closer to them. The house was crowded because Dante refused to stop caring for his half brother and half sisters. The three joined Dante, his wife, and their children under one roof. Dante gave them attention, as well as lodging. Any time he did not spend at work was devoted to his family. He took good care of all those who depended on him. Taking in his relatives was a kind and generous gesture, but it was expensive, too. Dante often had to borrow money from his wife's father in order to make ends meet. This tied him even closer to the Donatis at a time when they were quarreling with another influential family, the Cerchis. These two families stood at opposite ends of a growing rift within the Guelph Party.

The Guelphs had held sole power in Florence since 1266. During the next 33 years, there was never a challenge to Guelph authority. The Ghibelline threat had disappeared, and no other threats had appeared. In fact, as alternatives to Guelph rule evaporated, a substantial degree of consensus arose. The Guelphs were certainly happy. Yet when the opposition went away, so did the motivation for Guelph unity. As has so often happened in history, the Guelphs, with no outside enemies, started fighting among themselves. The Donatis and Cerchis chose opposite sides in the debate.

Disagreements and insults came first, but before long, insults turned into violence. Harsh words quickly gave way to fists, knives, and clubs. Families and clans lined up with one faction or another. The Donati and Cerchi families were transformed into warring camps. They aligned themselves with one or the other of what were fast becoming two small armies. Each of these armies acted the part, too. Arms were taken up, and alliances were made with other factions in other cities. The sides even chose colors for their groups. The Donatis signed on with what became known as the Black Guelphs. The Cerchis joined the White Guelphs. With so much antagonism and fear around, bitter accusations of treason were alleged by both sides. Open street warfare quickly followed, and blood flowed freely. "Hatred and enmities arose," one writer claimed, as "citizens rushed to arms . . . blinded by wrath. . . ."[34]

MAKING ENEMIES

Dante feared that Florence would be torn apart if something was not done to stop the bloodshed, and the other priors agreed. They supported Dante and, with him, stepped in to settle the dispute. Their first move was to exile the leadership of both sides. Top Donatis and Cerchis alike—those who comprised the leadership of the Guelph factions in Florence—were forced to leave Florence in disgrace. Getting rid of them, so the priors thought, would go a long way toward ending the larger conflict. They were right, but they did not anticipate the consequences. Dante especially, did not see what was coming. The actions the priors took made the city safer, but they also turned many people against Dante. Both sides held angry grudges against him. Even after he left office, influential Florentines remembered his role in chasing out the feuding Guelph leaders. They sought to ruin him, and when he became superintendent of roads in 1301, they got their chance.

Such a minor position as superintendent of roads might have put Dante beyond the reach of politics in many cities, but this was Florence; everything was political. While overseeing road construction and maintenance, Dante got into trouble. He was never afraid to comment on matters of state, and on one occasion, he was asked his opinion on whether or not to give military aid to Pope Boniface VIII during a nasty land dispute. Not completely thinking through his words, Dante recommended that Florence not help the pope. "About the papal matter," the official report read, "Dante Alighieri advised that nothing be done."[35] Eventually, Florentine officials aided the pope, despite the advice of Dante and others to the contrary. Pope Boniface accepted the assistance, but he never forgot the city's initial reluctance. He also neither forgot nor forgave Dante.

Pope Boniface was determined to get even. Sometime later, the pope learned of a French plan to attack Florence, and he quickly threw his support behind the operation. Led by its king, the French force entered Italy and promptly occupied Florence. The French wanted an Italian in charge, a man who would do what they wanted once they left. They chose Corso Donati, one of the very men Dante had helped to send into exile. Dante had humiliated Corso Donati, and the furious leader wanted revenge. In January 1302, Florence's government charged Dante with bribery and corruption. City officials accused him of stealing money that had been set aside for roads. The priors called Dante a thief.

BONIFAC[..] VS VIII
P·M·

This thirteenth-century portrait shows Pope Boniface VIII.
Dante got into trouble when he recommended that
Florence deny military aid to the pope.

Dante, of course, refused to respond to the charges. He would never dignify such absurd accusations with an answer. The city should be praising him, Dante thought, not leveling disgraceful accusations. He would not speak to such nonsense. Secretly, however, he was afraid.

Things only got worse. Frustrated by Dante's silence, city officials fined him and told him to leave. If the poet would not speak, he should go. Dante was banished. Branded a thief, he was driven out of the city he loved. The government had spoken. There was nothing he could do. Once more, just as it had been with his arranged marriage, Dante was forced give up what he loved because someone else told him to. Totally dispirited, Dante gathered what he could carry, and headed for Rome. He thought he might be able to pull himself together there, and perhaps find a way out of this mess. Dante was in Rome when a message arrived telling him he had been condemned to death. His actions—or lack of them—had sealed his fate. Dante's response to the corruption charges, or more to the point his silence, had convinced the priors that he was guilty. An innocent man, they reasoned, would have loudly

Pope Boniface VIII proclaims the First Jubilee (Holy Year) in 1300. The pope became a central figure in Dante's banishment from Florence.

proclaimed his innocence. Dante did not argue for his innocence, so the priors decided he must have been guilty all along. In his absence, the priors issued Dante's death warrant. The proud poet was informed that he would be burned alive if he ever returned to Florence.

The city of Dante's birth had turned on him. Florentine officials called him a criminal, drove him away, and now sentenced him to die. In exile, Dante had lost his second great love after Beatrice Portinari—Florence. Hiding in a strange city, he knew in his heart that he would never be able to return to his home. His political career in the service of Florence was finished. He had no true love, no city, and no political future. Dante, it seemed, once again had to begin a new life.

Test Your Knowledge

1 After the death of Beatrice Portinari, what did Dante do?
   a. He left Italy forever.
   b. He enlisted in the military.
   c. He began painting.
   d. He wrote *La Vita Nuova*.

2 Dante entered the world of politics by
   a. joining a local guild.
   b. running for mayor.
   c. soliciting votes for a friend.
   d. none of the above.

3 Which of the following best characterizes the political climate of Florence around 1300?
   a. A unified city of like-minded people
   b. A city of many factions and family feuds
   c. A dictatorship ruled by a single nobleman
   d. A communal society where labor and wealth were equally divided

4 How did Pope Boniface take out his grudge against Dante?
   a. He had Dante removed from political office.
   b. He had Dante's pay withheld.
   c. He backed a French invasion of Florence.
   d. He condemned Dante to hell.

5   How did Dante react to the corruption charges
    brought against him?
    a. With silence, resulting in his exile
    b. With an immediate confession
    c. With a plea bargain
    d. By raising his own private army

ANSWERS: 1. d; 2. a; 3. b; 4. c; 5. a

Wandering

Driven out of Florence, Dante drifted first to Rome, and then into the hill country of Tuscany, where he joined other Florentine exiles. These men were not like Dante, however. They were far from content, living outside the city walls of their hometown. They formed a conspiracy and pledged themselves to one another. All of the men with whom Dante joined wanted to go back to Florence, and they did not much care what they had to do to get there. If the city government would not let them return peacefully, they would do so by force. These former citizens, unlike their new friend, plotted a violent return home. As their scheme evolved, the men began to frighten Dante. He wanted nothing to do with any plan aimed at invading and seizing control of Florence. In addition, it was silly to think that such a move might work. Dante told his angry acquaintances to forget about it, but they kept preparing. Arguments followed. In the end, Dante's opposition to the conspiracy convinced the plotters to give up. The whole incident, however, bothered Dante. He chose to leave Tuscany and move on.

On the road again, Dante traveled first to Verona in northern Italy. Verona resembled Florence, both in its appearance and in its politics. Everyone had a political opinion in Verona. No one was neutral. People there, including the newly arrived Dante, had to choose sides in the ongoing White Guelph versus Black Guelph dispute. Dante, fearing a repeat of the Florence episode, reluctantly chose to side

A view of Florence from the countryside is shown here. Once exiled, Dante yearned for a city to become his new Florence.

with the Black Guelphs. He did not want to choose sides, but he felt he had no alternative. Angry at having to take any position at all, Dante lashed out at the White Guelphs. It was not like Dante to use harsh words, but after all he had been through, he was bitter and resentful. Dante called the White Guelphs "wicked and stupid . . . completely ungrateful, mad, and impious."[36] He declared himself independent of the White Guelphs, once and for all. He stormed out of Verona in a rage, before finally giving up on

Guelph politics altogether. He was fed up with both sides. He decided to make himself "a party of one."[37] Dante believed in serving the city, not in serving a particular group's vanity.

Alone again, Dante wandered from one place to another. He went to Padua and then to Bologna. Every place seemed so foreign. Wherever Dante set foot, he felt like a complete stranger. The only thing Dante wanted was a place to call home. He yearned for a city that could be his new Florence. Dante was exhausted by the time he stopped in Lucca. He was worn out, but he could still write—so he did.

THE WRITINGS OF A LIFETIME

First Dante put together a brief study of language and poetry in a book called *De Vulgari Eloquentia*. He praised all human languages, but none more so than Italian. Dante could have singled out Latin for special honors. Most other people at that time would have. Latin was the ancient language of the great Roman Empire. The Roman Catholic Church still used Latin, and scholars wrote in it almost exclusively. Europe relied on Latin to provide the words for its laws, edicts, treaties, and even academic

Verona

Dante drifted from place to place after he was sent into exile. It hurt him a great deal to be alone, unable to go home. Florence meant more to him than almost anything else, but he had been thrown out. Now he was desperate for a new home. His next city would have to have all of the charm and grace of Florence. He found just such a city in Verona. Verona was a beautiful little city that looked and felt just like Florence in many ways. It was walled, for one thing, and Verona had a river right in the middle of it, as did Florence. The city's buildings were lovely, and Verona's art was first-rate. Most important to Dante, the countryside beyond Verona's walls reminded him of the places he had known as a boy. The green fields and rolling hills outside Verona made Dante think of home, and the good old days. They brought back many happy memories. Verona was a very special place. In fact, if Dante closed his eyes, he could almost imagine himself back in Florence. Such pleasant thoughts made Dante smile, until he remembered what Florence had done to him. Verona was a good substitute for his real home, but Dante would not have been there, if Florence had not betrayed him. Even as he settled into life in Verona, Dante's heart ached.

degrees. It would have been logical for Dante to pick Latin over Italian, but he did not do so. Dante chose Italian, the daily language of the common people. It is unclear exactly why he did this, but the choice revealed Dante's love for his homeland. To him, nothing sounded as beautiful as Italian, and he wanted everyone else to be exposed to it. *Di Vulgari Eloquentia* was quite popular. In an instant, Dante became a truly Italian author. This time, he spoke not just for Florence but for all of Italy. "If the Italian language had been waiting for a voice, Dante gave it that voice."[38]

Eloquentia was just the start, however. Dante's next book, *Convivio,* gained him even more fame. It was an odd project for Dante. The book was supposed to be about poetry, but it went much farther. It became essentially a story about the author himself. *Convivio* was a tale of Dante's love for the Italian language and for the city of Florence. The work was upbeat, at least on the surface. Despite a seemingly positive theme, however, in many parts of the book, Dante expressed his anger and disappointment at being exiled. Some chapters contained outright protests against his treatment, and complaints about injustice. The very first part of the book, for example, was filled with expressions of resentment. Dante lamented his inability to find a home. He claimed that he had "unjustly suffered punishment . . . of exile and poverty." Florence had cruelly cast him out. "I have wandered through almost every region," he sadly noted, "a stranger, almost a beggar." Worse still, was the fact that Dante's reputation had been irreparably damaged. "Every work of mine," he remarked, "became of less esteem." [39]

Dante clearly felt betrayed by Florence, his friends, and life in general. His wanderings were not simply the result of poor political choices. Dante felt sure that he had been pushed out of Florence by evil men who were much less worthy than he. These so-called nobles and civic leaders had hurt him deeply, but in *Convivio*, Dante challenged Florence's elite. All they had was money, he suggested. None of his enemies possessed any real merit. They had riches, in short, but gold could not buy them virtue. Dante made his case to his readers in clear, forceful terms. He told them not to look for honor in wealth. "Nobility is wherever virtue is," Dante wrote. [40]

Writing allowed Dante Alighieri (shown here) to release some of the anger he felt toward the men of Florence who had played a role in his exile.

Exile had sharpened Dante's words. *Convivio* was the product of a man who had lost everything that had mattered most to him. He was a sad and lonely man, living like a nomad in his own land. Dante's writing came from the heart, however broken it might have been. Still he found some room for love in his heart and his work. Deep down, Dante still felt joy in his memories of Florence and Beatrice Portinari. Although she had died many years before, Dante still loved her just as much as he had when he was a boy. She was never far from his mind. In fact, the third part of *Convivio* contained a discussion of wisdom. Interestingly wisdom was portrayed as a woman. Dante spoke of wisdom in terms of divine love in a female form.

Clearly, Beatrice Portinari remained Dante's true love still. He appeared to be writing about philosophy, but he was really writing about his true love. He even went so far as to claim that his own words echoed in his head as he wrote. He kept hearing his own voice "speaking in my mind of my lady so reverently."[41] Dante was still very much in love with the pretty little girl he had met so long ago on that sunny day in May.

DESCENDING INTO THE INFERNO

The memory of Beatrice Portinari brought some measure of joy back into Dante's troubled life. She was gone, however, and no amount of fantasizing would ever bring her back. Similarly, Dante could never forget that Florence had forced him out. He could not have his one true love, and he could never go home. Dante accepted the fact that his painful exile would be permanent. As one of his biographers wrote years later, "all hope, though not the desire, of ever returning to Florence was gone."[42] Dante eventually came to peace with the reality of exile. Florence, "my city, that shuts me out from her," became for Dante just another lost love.[43] As with Beatrice Portinari, he would always miss Florence.

Dante could have ended his career at this point. He had put his personal anguish in the pages of his books, for the world to see. He could have stopped writing. He had said everything he needed to say. That would have been enough for most men, but not Dante. Something changed inside him. Instead of allowing him to get on with his life, the writing of *Convivio* actually made him feel worse than before.

By 1310, Dante had become even more resentful. Life had cheated him, so he came to believe. He did not deserve to be treated the way he had. Slowly Dante's attitude toward Florence turned hostile. The anger he had felt since being sent away began to boil inside him. Exile would not be the end of it, he told himself. It was only the beginning of a far greater story.

Dante began to write once more, this time with a vengeance. If banishment was the opening chapter, now he would finish the tale. With Florence and Beatrice Portinari on his mind, Dante sat down to write what emerged as his masterpiece. Dante said good-bye to the world that had caused him so much heartache, and said hello to *The Inferno*.

Test Your Knowledge

1 Where did Dante travel while in exile?

   a. Tuscany

   b. Verona

   c. Padua

   d. All of the above

2 Most of the other exiles that Dante met wanted to

   a. remain expatriates.

   b. become priests.

   c. return to Florence, at any cost.

   d. become Roman citizens.

3 What was *De Vulgari Eloquentia*?

   a. A dictionary

   b. A book of poems

   c. A diatribe against the leaders of
      Florence

   d. A book praising the Italian language

4 Although *Convivio* was supposed to be a
   book about poetry, it also contained

   a. bitter protests against Dante's treatment.

   b. a long play about the author's life.

   c. many biblical verses.

   d. all of the above.

5 After finishing *Convivio*, what did Dante decide to do?

a. End his life

b. Return to Florence and risk death

c. Stop writing altogether

d. Begin a new work based on his banishment

ANSWERS: 1. d; 2. c; 3. d; 4. a; 5. d

The Inferno

I n the spring of 1306, Dante was alone, lost, and bitter. His life seemed to be one long stream of disappointments and hardships. He blamed himself, in part, for some of his difficulties, but the real problem, he came to believe, was the corrupt world in which he lived. Dante came to believe that his bad fortune was the result of the work of evil men. Someday, he told himself, these villains would pay. So would Florence, a city that had given itself over to greed and treachery. Dante looked back on his home city and saw nothing but sin, and sin would be punished.

In this dark mood, Dante sat down to write his most famous book, *The Inferno*, which would mark the climax of his life and career. The book was really a three-part tale. It marked the appearance of "a new Dante," as one writer put it. In fact, Dante had undergone a total "change of heart . . . a turn to a religious view of man and his fate."[44] Dante, in other words, started thinking about politics in moral terms. Not only could individuals be good and bad, but entire cities, like Florence, could have a positive or negative character, as well. Dante was trying to show how ironic the human journey could be, so his new work was called *La Divina Commedia (Divine Comedy)*.

The finished product told the story of Dante's imaginary travels through hell, purgatory, and finally heaven. Each leg of the trip was described in a different story, or part, of the completed book. Each part, in turn, received a separate and appropriate title: part three was *Paradiso* (*Paradise*) and part two was *Purgatorio* (*Purgatory*). The first installment, entitled *The Inferno (Hell)*, became the best known book.

The Divine Comedy explored three separate, but related, stages in one man's lifelong effort to understand people better and come to know his God. The story also traced what Dante felt was the course of his life. He had been cast out of Florence; that was hell. Now he wandered between worlds; that was purgatory. In the end, Dante hoped with all his heart, he would return to a perfect city, in other words, heaven.

THE PIT

The trip from one place to another began in the fires of Satan's lair. Here Dante's writing and social criticism were at their sharpest. Dante, in *The Inferno*, flatly accused Florence of being a corrupt and sinful city. It was not always that way for Dante, but lately he had come to feel that Florence was controlled entirely by vicious men who were his enemies. It was these enemies, and other immoral sorts of people, whom he sentenced to

A scene from *The Inferno*, the third and most famous book of *The Divine Comedy*, is depicted here. For Dante, *The Inferno* came to represent the evil, corrupt men of Florence.

an eternity of pain and repentance in the pages of *The Inferno*.

The Inferno began right where Dante felt himself to be at that very moment—middle-aged and wandering. In the middle of his life's journey, the story's narrator said, "I found myself alone in dark woods, the right road lost." Confused and uneasy, the narrator felt the "old fear stirring: death is hardly more bitter." The tale he had to tell would be a sad one. The place he was at was not good. Yet the narrator promised his audience that he would go on. He would "tell what I saw" in the dark woods before him, even though, like Dante, he did not know when "it was I began to blunder off the true path."[45]

After this introduction, the narrator, joined by the famous Roman writer Virgil, went down into the depths of hell. The two travelers descended slowly, passing first through an ominous gateway. Above it was an inscription that read, "Through me you enter into the city of woes, Through me you enter into eternal pain, Through me you enter the population of loss. . . . Abandon all hope ye who enter here."[46]

Past this gloomy gate, the two men proceeded downward through the nine circles of hell. These nine levels of torment led from the earth to the home of Satan himself. Each succeeding level was occupied by sinners of increasing degree. With each step, in other words, the narrator and Virgil met up with men and women who had done things for which they were being punished. These hopeless people were assigned, by the devil, tortures that matched the degree of their crimes in life. The worse one's sins, the worse the punishment. There were many unfortunate inhabitants of the circles. Some were people whose only offense was to never have known God. Others were truly evil men who had betrayed their families, and, worse yet, their countries.

From the unlucky to the monstrous, Dante showed his readers all kinds of people who hurt society. Each step along the way, the men and women the narrator met described what they had done to earn their place in hell. These so-called "shades," named for the fact that they were ghosts of their former selves, also asked Dante about the people and places they had left behind. Many of these lost souls asked specifically about Florence. They quizzed the narrator about friends and relatives, and the happenings in the city. Like Dante, his characters were exiles. Like him, they could never go home. As the narrator passed through the circles, he realized this. With great sadness, he left all those people he encountered to their own painful fate.

From one circle to the next, Dante's protagonist saw, spoke to, and pitied the souls he met in hell, and they were a mixed bunch. Starting at the top, just below pagans who never knew God, the narrator met gluttons. These people stuffed themselves with food while others starved. He also met angry and sullen people who had hurt others with their vicious tempers and dark moods. The narrator passed violent souls who hurt themselves and others. He found along his way flatterers, hypocrites, and liars whose sweet words deceived everyone, except God. Down the narrator went, deeper and deeper, to the very lowest level of hell. Here he found the worst of the worst. At the bottom of the pit were traitors. These men had turned their backs on their homeland. They were subjected to the most terrifying tortures for their sins. They existed on a frozen plain, locked in ice. They suffered for all eternity in the constant company of Satan himself.

Dante's narrator found Satan at the heart of everything and everyone who made the world a terrible place. Portrayed in *The Inferno* as a three-faced giant, Satan ruled hell while frozen from the waist down in a sea of ice. Around him were other villains twisted and deformed by their sins. They surrounded Satan, "shades . . . covered wholly by ice . . . some lying prone, some erect, some with the head toward us and others with the bottoms of the feet; Another like a bow, bent feet to face."[47] Everyone was ruled by the hideous, fallen angel who "was once as beautiful as he is ugly now."[48] Leaving Satan and his followers in their torment, Dante's narrator exited hell. With that, he concluded his sad tale of sin and punishment.

UPWARD TOWARD A BETTER WORLD

Dante's ultimate purpose in writing *The Inferno* is a bit unclear, but he almost certainly expressed, at least in part, some of his own sorrow. His words and descriptions reflected the frustration and anger bottled up inside him. When he described hell as "the city of woes," he was referring to Florence. The inhabitants of that sinister place were obviously the people who drove him out and ruined his life. Taken together, they represent the Florentine citizenry. Although Dante loved Florence, he believed that evil people had destroyed it. Better to leave the place behind, Dante came to believe, just as his main character in *The Inferno* had left hell.

Dante did not give up all hope, however. The books that followed *The Inferno* put his narrator on

A Lake of Ice

Dante boiled with anger. He had given Florence all he had to give. He loved his city, and it had pushed him away. That was not entirely true, however. Dante knew that Florence was innocent. The city itself, after all, had done nothing. Dante's enemies were the men who had done all of the damage. A few rotten men had ruined his life, he imagined. Liars and cheats had betrayed him. Worse still, they had given Florence a bad name. Dante now wondered how to punish them—at least in the pages of the book he was writing. He wondered what Satan would do with such men in hell. Dante thought hard, and suddenly it came to him. Men who betrayed their the road to ultimate happiness. In *Purgatorio* and *Paradiso*, the main character climbed out of the fiery pit, and got to heaven. There the eternally beautiful Beatrice Portinari waited to take him to see God. By stages, then, Dante had the narrator move from loss and hopelessness to utter joy; from heartache to bliss. The narrator's journey was a life's journey that mirrored Dante's own life.

cities had a heart that felt no warmth. When they died, then, they would need a fitting home, one that would be just as frigid as their heart. Dante felt that his enemies deserved a place where even their insincere tears would freeze. So the final circle in hell was reserved for men who turned on their cities. Here these betrayers were encased in a sea of ice. Herded together, these wicked souls cried in agony. Yet each tear that ran down their disloyal cheeks froze. The tears fed the icy lake that held them all as prisoners. Hearts of ice in a sea of ice, Dante's mind had created an everlasting punishment for his enemies. Dante finally got his revenge.

An illustration of purgatory is shown here. In Dante's *Purgatorio,* the main character climbed out of the fiery pit, and got to heaven.

Dante hoped that the story he wrote would become his reality. He yearned to leave behind his loneliness and exile, and to be reunited with Florence and his true love, Beatrice. Florence, if all went well, would someday be cleansed of all of its sins and deceit. Perhaps then, just as the narrator eventually reached heaven, Dante could go home. Maybe then, he could feel once more the warmth of what he called "*la carità del natio loco* [love of my native city]."[49] Sadly Dante's hopes were not to be fulfilled. Beatrice Portinari was dead and Florence was closed to him forever. Imaginary journeys from hell to heaven could not change the facts. As Dante finished his magnificent trilogy, he began to live out the final chapter of his life.

Test Your Knowledge

1 Who did Dante blame most for his hardships?

a. The Catholic Church

b. The corrupt world

c. Beatrice Portinari

d. His father

2 Which book begins Dante's *Divine Comedy*?

a. *Paradiso*

b. *Commedia*

c. *Purgatorio*

d. *Inferno*

3 Where does *The Divine Comedy* begin?

a. In heaven

b. In hell

c. In Florence

d. In Rome

4 According to Dante's work, how many circles of hell are there?

a. Five

b. Three

c. Nine

d. Seven

5 According to *The Inferno*, who occupies the lowest level of hell?

a. Murderers

b. Corrupt politicians

c. The Roman poet Virgil

d. Traitors

ANSWERS: 1. b; 2. d; 3. b; 4. c; 5. d

A Life's Journey Ended

Dante Alighieri wrote furiously for 14 years, before he finished his *Divine Comedy* in 1320. Seemingly sensing that his life was drawing to a close, he scribbled urgently. Still Dante made time for a life away from his writing. That part of his world was dominated by a burning desire to end his exile. Dante longed to complete his own personal journey from hell to heaven by returning to Florence. If he had only a brief time remaining to live, Dante wanted that time to be spent in the city he loved. As he approached the end of his days, nothing occupied a more important place in his mind and heart.

The concluding chapter of Dante's story opened in the spring of 1315. Dante was in Verona working on *Purgatorio,* when bad news arrived. Dante had suffered so much, and most of his problems had revolved around his relationship with Florence. He was angry at the city, but it was still, in an odd sense, dear to him. He felt a great sense of uneasiness when news reached Verona that Florence was under attack. The city was threatened by forces commanded by a rebellious local nobleman. The call went out for every able-bodied Florentine to rush to the aid of the city. Even exiles, like Dante, were called home. Dante would have loved to fight for Florence once again, but he was still living under a sentence of death should he ever return to the city. No matter how badly he wanted to defend his birthplace, he did not dare show his face. Florence's government, at this point, offered a solution: Dante

In writing *The Divine Comedy*, Dante hoped that he would some day be reunited in heaven with Beatrice Portinari, his true love. The meeting between Beatrice and Dante is illustrated here.

could come home anytime, if he paid a fine and admitted that he was guilty of the crimes that had gotten him exiled. Dante was promised that, if he begged for forgiveness in a church, he would be allowed to join Florence's army.

Dante was too proud to accept the conditions offered. He was, in fact, deeply insulted. He called the city's demands "ridiculous." He told a friend that he had no intention of allowing "himself to be presented at the altar as a prisoner." Dante asked, "Is this the glorious recall whereby Dante Alighieri is summoned back to the fatherland after suffering almost fifteen years of exile?"[50] He brushed aside Florence's offer of a pardon. He refused to give it even a single moment of thought. It hurt him to be called back like some sort of fugitive from justice. He had done nothing wrong in the first place. He certainly did not need the city's forgiveness now. Florence, as far as he was concerned, could fight its own battles, and it could do so without the help of Dante Alighieri.

Florence's ruling council was furious. Its leaders fumed at the idea that Dante would refuse an offer as generous as theirs. Worse yet, he did so while still maintaining his innocence. The government issued an order calling for everything the Alighieris owned to be taken away. It also approved the arrest and execution of Dante's sons, as the children of a traitor. Luckily the warrant was never successfully served, but its mere existence was an unmistakable sign to Dante. His relationship with Florence was over—permanently. The city was dead to him. From now on, home was wherever Dante chose to wander.

ONE LAST JOB

Confirmed in his exile, Dante left Verona. He drifted around from place to place, until at last, he ended up in the city of Ravenna. Not too long after he settled down, Dante was joined by his wife and his daughter Antonia. It was a real comfort to have at least part of his family with him. The company helped to ease his pain, and exile became a little bit more tolerable.

Consoled by his wife and daughter, once again Dante focused his energies on writing. Day and night, he put words down on paper. It was a feverish and productive period of work. Dante's only distraction came when he was asked to make an effort in diplomacy. Ravenna and the city of Venice had a longstanding dispute. Most of the Italian city-states had fought their neighbors at one time or another. A few seemed to go to war against each other routinely. They almost became accustomed to it. Lasting damage was rarely done, but this time, things were different. War between Ravenna and Venice promised to be bloody, and no one wanted that. Ravenna decided to send a peace envoy to Venice, with the hope that the envoy would defuse the situation, allowing everybody to calm down. Whoever took the job would have to be clear-headed and sensible. He would have to be good with words, a natural negotiator. Ravenna asked Dante Alighieri to be that man.

Dante, as one writer put it, "gladly accepted the charge" of going to Venice to seek peace.[51] In his heart, Dante had always wanted to avoid conflict. He had never asked for any of the troubles he had encountered in Florence. He eagerly accepted the opportunity to smooth out the problems between Ravenna and Venice, but he would have to act quickly. There was no time to waste. In fact, Venice declared war on Ravenna before he could even leave on his mission. Very soon the fighting would begin. The Venetians, "confident in their strength and power," had, at that moment, launched a huge fleet of ships toward Ravenna. Dante's job suddenly got harder, as the stakes in the contest rose.

Dante, at first, had thought only about the details of the upcoming negotiations. Real lives were at stake. If he could not bring peace, many people were going to die. He could not fail. Hundreds, maybe thousands, of lives depended on his success. He could feel the stress growing. He worried constantly that he might not "be able to turn aside the impending ruin." He worried that he might disappoint the people of Ravenna. Every day, every hour, he became more nervous. As the strain grew, his health began to suffer. Some people believe that the job of settling the quarrel between Ravenna and Venice actually "hastened the death of the poet."[52]

THE END OF A POETIC LIFE

Stressed to near his breaking point, Dante left for Venice, where he received a very cool greeting. Although he was a Florentine, the Venetians looked

Making Memories

After Dante's death, his son Piero worked hard to live up to his father's memory. He went to school and studied very hard. Eventually Piero became a lawyer. Like his father, Piero Alighieri loved Verona. Also like his father, who had served Florence and later Ravenna, Piero gave Verona all the time and energy he could. He led an active civic life, and got married. When his first son was born, he named him Dante. The new Dante Alighieri also lived a life that would have made his namesake proud. His son, Lionardo, went out of his way to keep his great-grandfather's memory alive. Lionardo Alighieri even visited Florence, and took time to visit with his illustrious ancestor's biographer, a writer named Giovanni Boccaccio. Lionardo Alighieri wanted to learn as much as he could about his great-grandfather. Boccaccio took the curious young man from one place to another. The biographer showed him the spots where Dante Alighieri had lived and worked. He told Lionardo Alighieri everything he wanted to know. Boccaccio gave Lionardo Alighieri a real sense of how "Fortune turns this world," and how fate governed Dante's days.*

* Lionardo Bruno Aretino, *The Life of Dante,* in *The Earliest Lives of Dante.* New York: Frederick Ungar Publishing Company, 1963, p. 95.

at Dante as if he were a native of Ravenna. He was literally the enemy. In addition, he was renowned for his speaking ability. Everyone knew how persuasive Dante could be. Few people had ever heard him speak without being swayed by his logic and reasoning. The Venetians were well aware of his skills. They were concerned that he might convince them to recall the forces they had sent to attack Ravenna. Being "little trained in eloquence," the Venetians "feared the man." They did not want to be "shaken in their proud purpose" by Dante's words. Venice wanted war, and was afraid that Dante might produce peace.[53]

The Venetian rulers responded by refusing to even listen to Dante. "Though Dante begged again and again" to speak with them, the Venetians "refused to give him an audience."[54] After repeated attempts to present his side had failed, Dante decided to go home. Once again, however, he was disappointed. The Venetians would not let him board a ship for Ravenna because of the war. Dante lingered for a few days, and then asked for permission to depart by land. The Venetians gave in, and let him go.

Dante's trip back to Ravenna was boring. There was little to look at and nothing to do. The worst part of the journey was traveling through the awful marshes that lined the road. Shallow, stagnant, and smelly, the marshes were home to clouds of buzzing mosquitoes that swarmed everywhere. The little insects needed blood, and they would take it from any animal or person that happened to be around. At that moment, a tiny mosquito bit Dante as he rode through the stinking swamp. In its saliva, the mosquito carried the parasite that caused malaria, and Dante was infected with the disease.

The small bump left behind by the mosquito must have itched a bit, but Dante gave it no thought. By the time he arrived in Ravenna, however, he was feeling quite ill. He weakened, and within a few days he collapsed, burning with fever. He suffered tremendously. The pain, chills, sweating, and muscle spasms common to malaria made Dante miserable. He was in pain, but he had never given up on anything in his life, and he would not start now. He fought the deadly disease with all his might and courage. Nature, however, won in the end.

In the final moments of Dante's life, a priest came to his bedside to offer last rites. Perhaps Dante's bedroom looked something like this replica of a bedroom from the Palazzo Davanzati in Florence.

Dante knew he was dying. Shaking with fever, he called for a priest to come and give him his last rites. A priest came to Dante's bedside and passed on God's forgiveness for all of the poet's earthly sins. His soul was cleansed and made ready to meet God. There would be no inferno for Dante. His heart was lightened by the priest's words, and by the knowledge that he would soon be in heaven with Beatrice Portinari. Yes, just as she had led the narrator in *Paradiso* into heaven, she would be there when Dante arrived. Death lost its sting when Dante thought of an eternity with his true love. Calmly, and with the certainty that he would be "received in the arms of his most noble Beatrice," the writer began to slip away.[55] Dante Alighieri died quietly on September 14, 1321.

Italy lost its most able writer that day. People mourned, but they found comfort in the belief that Dante's troubled soul had gone on to a much better place. Dante's "weary spirit" had "left behind the miseries of the present life." The gracious Florentine, who had loved Italy and its language with all his heart, so a later biographer wrote, went on to live forever "most blissfully in that life [in which] we believe there is no end."[56]

Test Your Knowledge

1 What would Dante have had to do to gain a pardon from Florence?

　a. Pay a fine.

　b. Admit to crimes.

　c. Beg forgiveness in a church.

　d. All of the above

2 Who joined Dante in Ravenna?

　a. His former tutor, Brunetto Latini

　b. His wife and daughter

　c. A friend from his exile in Tuscany

　d. The pope

3 Dante's last job was as

　a. envoy from Ravenna to Venice.

　b. creator of a new form of poetry.

　c. field hand at a Ravenna orchard.

　d. none of the above.

4 How was Dante received in Venice?

　a. Like a king

　b. As a traitor

　c. The Venetians refused to see him at all.

　d. The Venetians were swayed toward peace by Dante's words.

5 Dante's death was the result of

a. a soldier's sword.

b. a small, infected cut on his hand.

c. malaria from a mosquito bite.

d. suicide.

ANSWERS: 1. d; 2. b; 3. a; 4. c; 5. c

Reading the
Pages of Dante

Dante Alighieri's books spoke to, and for, an Italy that was just beginning to rediscover itself. After centuries of silence, Italian citizens wanted their voices to be heard again. When the stagnation and disorder brought on by the fall of Rome began to clear, Italy's people began to seek new ways to express themselves.

They looked for ways to tell people what it meant to live in such a beautiful place, but they also realized that not everything was perfect. They saw the corruption around them. They feared the violence that pulled Italy into the ways of the past. Italians knew that it would take a lot of work to make their homeland strong, secure, and prosperous, but they believed that they were ready to take on the challenge.

Perhaps no other person in history expressed this fresh Italian spirit as well as Dante Alighieri. His words reflected a special moment in time. His books served as wonderful examples of the hopes, dreams, and concerns that most Italians shared during the early Renaissance. Dante's words were driven by a powerful new Italian identity. Although the peninsula would not be politically united until 1870, Dante helped Italians to develop a collective sense of self. In short, Dante Alighieri helped to revive Italy and make it proud. He represented the best that the Italian Renaissance had to offer Europe, and the rest of the world.

As is true of most great artists, poets, and writers, Dante Alighieri lived and created on two levels. On one level, he was openly political. His city,

In a scene from *The Inferno*, one of the three books of Dante's *Divine Comedy*, Virgil, Dante's Roman guide, appears to Dante in the woods. Virgil guided Dante through hell and purgatory, before ending the journey in heaven.

community, and country were very important to him. On another level, he was a thoroughly private person. He worked publicly for Italy, in particular Florence, while keeping his deepest emotions well hidden. The two aspects of Dante merged at only one point. His devotion to Florence and his love for Beatrice Portinari brought his two halves together. The man and his world blended, each mirroring the other. The strongest parts of each complemented the other, helping to make Dante Alighieri the great Italian writer that he became. His work revealed how a person can live his or her life as both a citizen and an individual. Dante showed that a person's private and public worlds could be compatible.

Dante's books took into account both the heart and the mind. Reading his masterpiece *La Divina Commedia* is almost like reading a political auto-biography. The narrator, Dante himself, moved from one stage of his life to another. He suffered pain, but learned how to move past it. In *The Inferno*, his public life collapsed and his private life was surrounded by torment. Still the narrator pressed on. He recognized how fortunate he was to avoid the fate of the souls who could never escape from the pit. The political

Dante punished his enemies and then left them to suffer their fate, but it was not an easy exit. Dante still struggled to escape his own personal hell created by his exile and the death of Beatrice Portinari.

In the end, the narrator did escape. He climbed higher and higher, leaving all of his political and personal problems behind. Along with the narrator, Dante passed through a time where life got better. He discovered a political life beyond Florence. He also learned to live with the loss of his true love, Beatrice Portinari. Dante, in the guise of the narrator, finally made his way to paradise. Heaven is where all of his problems were solved. It was the perfect "city," filled with honest men, much like him. More important, it was in heaven that the narrator found love once again, in the angelic form of Beatrice Portinari. It was perhaps fitting that Dante died so soon after completing *La Divina Commedia*. His real-life journey ended not long after his imaginary journey ended on paper.

Dante's other great books also blended political or cultural issues into his private world. *La Vita Nuova* and *Di Vulgari Eloquentia* are two good examples of this. In one, Dante set an agenda for a

Dante and Virgil (left) are shown with Francesca and Paolo (right), characters from *The Divine Comedy*. Dante died soon after completing *The Divine Comedy*.

professional and personal life after Beatrice Portinari. In the other, he envisioned a cultural universe spinning around a newly invigorated Italy. The books seemed to head in different directions, but were really very similar. *Di Vulgari* was an expression of both personal and private devotion, not just to Florence, but also to civic duty in general. Dante understood civic duty to mean political activity aimed at making society better. Participation in the political system of the city was supremely important to him. Through participation, the community as a whole could be improved. Dante, like many other Italians of his day, was convinced that ordinary men and women could transform the world. Life could be better, and average people could do their part to make it so. Individual virtue and goodness benefited

Florence: A City in Shame

Not long after Dante Alighieri died, Giovanni Boccaccio wrote the poet's biography. He followed Dante's life story very closely. At one point in his book, Boccaccio took time to scold the city of Florence for what it had done to Dante. According to Boccaccio, Florence had never deserved a loving son, such as Dante. The city, Boccaccio thought, should be ashamed of itself. It had exiled one of its best and truest citizens. For that, Florence would always be remembered as a failed and flawed city. Florence, he wrote, "I cannot escape being ashamed on your behalf."* Dante's "exile was a long one," Boccaccio said. The great poet "always called himself, and wished to be called, a Florentine . . .

everyone. Dante wanted his readers to think about their entire city, not just themselves.

In *La Vita Nuova*, Dante wrote about an existence beyond politics, but still linked to it. Even when he wrote about politics, his personal experiences came through. His love for Florence mixed with his love for Beatrice Portinari. His works often talked about politics in terms of beauty and harmony, exactly the

ever he loved you."** Dante had lived his life for himself, to be sure. Like most people, he had looked out for himself in a world that could be very unforgiving. Still, he had devoted his public talents to Florence. Boccaccio now accused that same city of ignoring the very special person it had sent away. Whatever happened to the city from then on, Boccaccio wrote, it had already had its chance at greatness. In rejecting Dante, Florence had rejected itself. Boccaccio reminded Florentines that something unique and timeless died with Dante.

* Giovanni Boccaccio, *The Life of Dante* in *The Earliest Lives of Dante*. New York: Frederick Ungar Publishing Company, 1963, p. 39.

** Ibid.

qualities he saw in Beatrice. In many ways, Dante's lifelong devotion to Beatrice Portinari guided his writing, regardless of the topic. Beatrice Portinari, or at least her influence, imparted a certain sense of warmth and hope into everything Dante wrote. Politics and passion, duty and love—they were all related for Dante Alighieri.

As an author, Dante is justly considered one of the world's greatest. Many people tried to follow his lead, but found it impossible to copy him. Dante has been compared to a mountain that towers over all its companions and rivals. "Dante's thought," one twentieth-century critic wrote, "stands among many chains and ridges . . . rising above them, shining in the sun."[57] Dante's power was in his willingness to blend the public and private, to make his work real, and of real value. The gift he left to the modern world is in the example of his life and work. He showed us how to bring the people and the community together into a seamless whole. He taught us how to create a social model where people took care of the community, and the community supported the people. In reality, of course, this ideal is difficult to realize. People today, as in Dante's time, are often more interested in caring for themselves. Still Dante challenged us to try, as he did. Strive to live a better life for yourself, he seemed to say in his writing, and make an effort to improve your community. Dante, in this way, left behind a lasting legacy that pointed later generations in the direction of a healthier society.

Dante showed how honest, virtuous people might contribute to their world, their nation, and their community. Ordinary men and women, boys and girls, could make life better, while at the same time, keeping their independence. Working for one's community does not mean sacrificing one's personal life. Nothing is lost, in other words, in the process of becoming an active citizen. Being a concerned and thoughtful member of society does not mean that a person has to become less of an individual. The world becomes a healthier, happier place for everyone when honest, honorable people take an ongoing interest in its progress. Good people, who do not let failure and disappointment stop them, improve all our lives. When someone can suffer tremendous loss and still keep giving to society, everyone benefits. Dante Alighieri proved that.

Test Your Knowledge

1 What did Dante's work give to the Italian
   people?
   a. A sense of national identity
   b. A collective sense of self
   c. A voice rising out of disorder
   d. All of the above

2 Dante's political life was characterized by
   a. his role as a peacemaker.
   b. betrayals and resentments.
   c. his role in the Catholic Church.
   d. a rapid rise to power over Florence.

3 Where did Dante get his inspiration for
   The Divine Comedy?
   a. Scandals in France
   b. The Catholic Church
   c. His own life experience
   d. His imagination alone

4 Dante was able to blend his personal and
   public life through
   a. his love for Beatrice Portinari.
   b. his writing.
   c. his journey through hell.
   d. none of the above.

5 Dante is best remembered as

   a. one of the world's greatest writers.

   b. a crafty politician.

   c. a bitter and defeated man.

   d. a brave soldier.

ANSWERS: 1. d; 2. b; 3. c; 4. b; 5. a

1265 Dante Alighieri is born in Florence.

1266 The Guelphs take power in Florence.

1272 Bella Alighieri, Dante's mother, dies suddenly.

1274 Dante meets Beatrice Portinari, his first love.

1281 Alighiero Alighieri, Dante's father, dies, leaving the young boy in charge of the Alighieri family.

1285 Fulfilling an eight-year-old contract for an arranged marriage, Dante takes Gemma Donati as his wife.

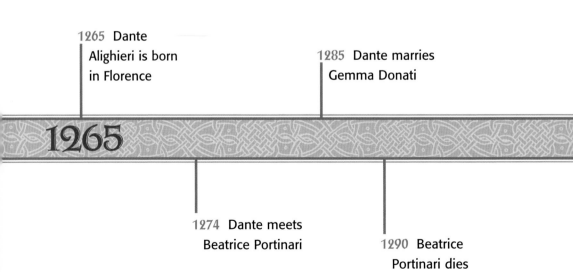

1265 Dante Alighieri is born in Florence

1285 Dante marries Gemma Donati

1265

1274 Dante meets Beatrice Portinari

1290 Beatrice Portinari dies

1289 At the Battle of Campaldino, Dante gains the military experience expected of a proper Florentine citizen.

1290 The death of Beatrice Portinari becomes the second tragedy in Dante's life; he writes *La Vita Nuova* (*The New Life*) in response.

1295 Dante joins a guild and begins his political career.

1300 Dante is elected as one of Florence's priors, or governors.

1301 After serving as prior, Dante takes a job as superintendent of roads.

1302 Dante is sent into exile based on false charges of corruprion

1321 Dante Alighieri dies

1325

1300 Dante is elected prior

1306–1320 Dante writes *La Divina Commedia* (*The Divine Comedy*)

1302   Enemies that Dante made during his time as prior take their revenge; Dante is sent into exile, based on false charges of corruption; next to the death of Beatrice Portinari, nothing hurt Dante more than being thrown out of the city he loved; in exile, Dante writes many books and breaks his longtime ties with the Guelph Party.

1306–1320   Dante outlines his image of the world, and his life, in the pages of the three-volume *La Divina Commedia* (*The Divine Comedy*); *The Inferno* becomes the most famous of the three books in the series.

1321   Dante Alighieri dies of malaria after trying to negotiate peace between Venice and his adopted city, Ravenna.

NOTES

CHAPTER 1:
The Flames of Hell, the Promise
of Paradise

1. Robert Pinsky, *The Inferno of Dante*. New York: Farrar, Straus and Giroux, 1994, p. 5.
2. Ibid., p. 7.
3. Ibid., p. 9.
4. Ibid., pp. 9–11.
5. Ibid., p. 11.
6. Giovanni Boccaccio, *Life of Dante* in *Earliest Lives of Dante*. New York: Frederick Ungar Publishing Company, 1963, p. 15.

CHAPTER 2:
Dante's Italy

7. Lauro Martinez, *Power and Imagination: City-States in Renaissance Italy*. Baltimore, MD: Johns Hopkins University Press, 1988, p. 24.
8. Charles Eliot Norton, "The Intellectual and Moral Awakening of Italy," *Aids to the Study of Dante,* ed. Charles Allen Dinsmore. New York: Houghton Mifflin Company, 1903, p. 49.
9. Ibid.
10. Dean Church, "Florentine Political Feuds and Their Influence on Dante," *Aids to the Study of Dante*, pp. 17–18.
11. Dante Alighieri, *Inferno,* trans. Robert and Jean Hollandar. New York: Anchor Books, 2000, p. xxv.

12. R.W.B Lewis, *Dante*. New York: Penguin Putnum, 2001, p. 22.
13. Donald E. Queller, *The Venetian Patriciate: Reality versus Myth*. Chicago: University of Illinois Press, 1986, p. 17.

CHAPTER 3:
A Birth in Florence

14. Boccaccio, *Life of Dante*, p. 15.
15. Ibid., p. 14.
16. Lewis, *Dante*, p. 25.
17. Boccaccio, *Life of Dante*, p. 19.
18. Lewis, *Dante*, p. 24.
19. Lionardo Bruni Aretino, *Life of Dante*, in *Earliest Lives of Dante*, p. 83.
20. Boccaccio, *Life of Dante*, p. 44.

CHAPTER 4:
From Boyhood to Manhood

21. Boccaccio, *Life of Dante*, pp. 42–43.
22. Lewis, *Dante,* p. 36.
23. Ibid., p. 28.
24. Boccaccio, *Life of Dante*, p. 45.
25. Lewis, *Dante*, p. 42.
26. Aretino, *Life of Dante*, in *Earliest Lives of Dante*, p. 83.

CHAPTER 5:
A Civic Life

27. Lewis, *Dante,* p. 46.
28. Boccaccio, *Life of Dante*, p. 20.
29. Ibid.
30. Lewis, *Dante*, p. 61.
31. Ibid., p. 69.
32. Boccaccio, *Life of Dante*, p. 27.
33. Aretino, *Life of Dante*, in *Earliest Lives of Dante*, p. 85.

34. Boccaccio, *Life of Dante*, p. 27.
35. Lewis, *Dante*, p. 80.

CHAPTER 6:
Wandering

36. Lewis, *Dante*, p. 89.
37. Ibid.
38. Aleghieri, *Inferno*, p. xxvii.
39. Lewis, *Dante*, p. 96.
40. Ibid., p. 99.
41. Ibid., p. 98.
42. Boccaccio, *Life of Dante*, p. 34.
43. Lewis, *Dante*, p. 100.

CHAPTER 7:
The Inferno

44. Lewis, *Dante*, p. 101.
45. Pinsky, *Inferno of Dante*, p. 5.
46. Ibid., p. 25.
47. Ibid., p. 365.
48. Ibid., p. 367.
49. Leo Spitzer, "Speech and Language in Inferno XIII," in *Dante: A Collection of Critical Essays*, ed. John Freccero. Englewood Cliffs, NJ: Prentice-Hall, 1965, p. 98.

CHAPTER 8:
A Life's Journey Ended

50. Lewis, *Dante*, p. 161.
51. Filippo Villani, "The Embassy to Venice," in *Earliest Lives of Dante*, p. 99.
52. Ibid.
53. Ibid.
54. Ibid.
55. Boccaccio, *Life of Dante*, p. 35.
56. Ibid.

CHAPTER 9:
Reading the Pages of Dante

57. Bruno Nardi, "Dante and Medieval Culture," in *Dante: A Collection of Critical Essays*, p. 42.

Alighieri, Dante. *Inferno*. Robert and Jean Hollander, trans. New York: Anchor Books, 2000.

Aretino, Lionardo Bruni. *Life of Dante* in *Earliest Lives of Dante*. New York: Frederick Ungar Publishing Company, 1963.

Boccaccio, Giovanni. *Life of Dante* in *Earliest Lives of Dante*. New York: Frederick Ungar Publishing Company, 1963.

Church, Dean "Florentine Political Feuds and Their Influence on Dante," in *Aids to the Study of Dante*. Charles Allen Dinsmore, ed. New York: Houghton Mifflin Company, 1903.

Lewis, R.W.B. *Dante*. New York: Penguin Putnum, 2001.

Martinez, Lauro. *Power and Imagination: City-States in Renaissance Italy*. Baltimore, MD: Johns Hopkins University Press, 1988.

Nardi, Bruno. "Dante and Medieval Culture." in *Dante: A Collection of Critical Essays*. John Freccero, ed. Englewood Cliffs, NJ: Prentice-Hall, 1965.

Norton, Charles Eliot "The Intellectual and Moral Awakening of Italy," in *Aids to the Study of Dante*. Charles Allen Dinsmore, ed. New York: Houghton Mifflin Company, 1903.

Pinsky, Robert. *The Inferno of Dante*. New York: Farrar, Straus and Giroux, 1994.

Queller, Donald E. *The Venetian Patriciate: Reality versus Myth*. Chicago: University of Illinois Press, 1986.

Spitzer, Leo. "Speech and Language in Inferno XIII," in *Dante: A Collection of Critical Essays*. John Freccero, ed. Englewood Cliffs, NJ: Prentice-Hall, 1965.

Villani, Filippo. "A Passage from *Life of Dante*," in *Earliest Lives of Dante*, New York: Frederick Ungar Publishing Company, 1963.

Books

Bloom, Harold. *Dante's Divine Comedy.* Philadelphia: Chelsea House Publishing, 2002.

Heuston, Kimberly. *Dante's Daughter.* Ashville, NC: Front Street Press, 2003.

Hollander, Robert. *Dante: A Life in Works.* New Haven, CT: Yale University Press, 2001.

Rubin, Harriet. *Dante in Love: The World's Greatest Poem and How it Made History.* NewYork: Simon & Schuster, 2004.

Tusiani, Joseph. *Dante's Divine Comedy: As Told for Young People.* Ottawa, Ontario, Canada: Legas Publishing, 2001.

Websites

Chronology of Dante Alighieri (1265–1321)
http://www.italnet.nd.edu/Dante/text/Chronology.html

Dante Alighieri (1265–1321): The Divine Comedy
http://jade.ccccd.edu/Andrade/WorldLitl2332/Dante/dante/DanteHomePage.html

Dante's The Divine Comedy
http://www.arches.uga.edu/~redman/

Everyday Life in Dante's Time
http://www.gpc.edu/~shale/humanities/literature/world_literature/dante/everyday.html

The World of Dante
http://www.iath.virginia.edu/dante/

page:

3: © Erich Lessing/Art Resource, NY

6: © Giraudon/Art Resource, NY

19: © Alinari/Art Resource, NY

25: © Bildarchiv Preussischer Kulturbesitz/Art Resource, NY

32: © Scala/Art Resource, NY

41: © Timothy McCarthy/Art Resource, NY

52: © Scala/Art Resource, NY

54: © Alinari Archives/CORBIS

69: © Archivo Iconografico, S.A./CORBIS

71: © Scala/Art Resource, NY

77: © Arte & Immagini srl/CORBIS

82: © Scala/Art Resource, NY

91: © Giraudon/Art Resource, NY

98: © Scala/Art Resource, NY

104: © Giraudon/Art Resource, NY

112: © Erich Lessing/Art Resource, NY

118: © SEF/Art Resource, NY

121: © SEF/Art Resource, NY

Cover: © Scala/Art Resource, NY

John C. Davenport holds a Ph.D. from the University of Connecticut and currently teaches at Corte Madera School in Portola Valley, California. Davenport is the author of several other books, including biographies of the Muslim leader Saladin and the writer C.S. Lewis. He lives in San Carlos, California, with his wife, Jennifer, and his two sons, William and Andrew.